Native American Life

Wickiups

by June Preszler

Consultant:
Leland M. Roth
Marion Dean Ross Distinguished Professor of Architectural History
Department of Art History, University of Oregon
Eugene, Oregon

Mankato, Minnesota

Bridgestone Books are published by Capstone Press,
151 Good Counsel Drive, P.O. Box 669, Mankato, Minnesota 56002.
www.capstonepress.com

Library of Congress Cataloging-in-Publication Data
Preszler, June, 1954–
Wickiups / by June Preszler.
    p. cm.—(Bridgestone books. Native American life)
    Includes bibliographical references and index.
    ISBN 0-7368-3728-0 (hardcover)
    1. Wickiups. 2. Indians of North America—Dwellings. I. Title. II. Series: Bridgestone Books:
Native American life (Mankato, Minn.)
E98.D9P744 2005
690'.8'08997—dc22   2004012403

Summary: A brief introduction to wickiups, including the materials, construction, and people who lived
    in these traditional Native American dwellings.

Editorial Credits
Katy Kudela, editor; Jennifer Bergstrom, designer; Kelly Garvin, photo researcher;
    Scott Thoms, photo editor

Photo Credits
The Denver Public Library, 6, 14, 16
Eda Rogers, 12, 18
James P. Rowan, 1
Library of Congress/Edward S. Curtis, 20
Marilyn "Angel" Wynn, cover, 4, 10
Smithsonian Institution, National Anthropological Archives, Negative 04518, 8

1 2 3 4 5 6 10 09 08 07 06 05

Table of Contents

4

What Is a Wickiup?

Wickiups are simple dome-shaped shelters. Native Americans built these huts out of wood, grass, and brush.

Native Americans who used wickiups often moved their camps. They crossed large areas during the year in search of food. Wickiups were simple shelters that were easy to build. When people moved, they could leave the wickiups behind.

◄ Some wickiups looked like a grass hut.

Who Lived in a Wickiup?

Wickiups were common among **tribes** in the western United States. The Paiute, Ute, and Shoshone lived in a large desert region called the **Great Basin**. They lived off the land hunting and gathering food. They moved in small groups called **bands**.

The Apache sometimes used wickiups. This Southwest tribe moved often to search for food.

Tribes today do not live in wickiups. They no longer need to travel in search of food.

◀ Some Apache lived in wickiups. This photograph shows an Apache camp in Arizona in the late 1800s.

Gathering Materials

The Great Basin Indians built wickiups from whatever materials they could find. They searched the land for brush, grass, and wood.

Builders looked for willow or oak saplings. They cut the wood to make poles for the **frame** of the wickiup.

People gathered plants. They needed grass and brush to cover the outside of the wickiup. They twisted reeds or strips of bark together to make **twine**.

◄ People gathered whatever wood they could find. They used the wood for shelters and cooking fires.

Preparing the Site

Women often built the wickiups. They first found a good place to build their shelters and then gathered materials.

Builders picked an area with flat ground. They drew a circle to mark where they would build the wickiup. People dug a small trench around the circle. They brought tree poles, branches, and grasses they gathered to the site.

◄ Flat, dry ground made a good place to build a wickiup.

Building a Wickiup

Builders first built the wickiup's frame. They stood thin poles in the trench. Once the poles were in place, builders bent the tops of the poles inward. They tied the poles at the top with twine. Next, they covered the frame with grass, brush, or branches. They left an opening at the front of the wickiup for a doorway.

Wickiups had a fire pit in the center. Builders left a small hole at the top of the wickiup to let out smoke.

◀ Tall grasses covered the frame of the wickiup.

Inside a Wickiup

Wickiups were very dark inside. The wickiup's only openings were the smoke hole and doorway.

People did not spend much time inside their wickiups. Families used wickiups as a place to sleep. They cooked and did other daily tasks outside. If the weather was very cold or wet, they sometimes stayed inside. The wickiup provided a warm shelter.

◄ A hunter built a wickiup for a place to sleep. This 1874 photograph shows a Paiute man in his wickiup.

Wickiup Villages

When bands found a hunting spot, they formed a **temporary** village. They quickly built wickiups. Sometimes they built as many as 15 in one day.

People built their wickiups in different sizes. Some were only large enough to hold one hunter. Others could hold a family.

When they couldn't find any more food, people moved to a new area. Most people left their wickiups behind. Sometimes, hunters would take their wickiups with them.

◄ People in a band built their wickiups close together and formed a village.

Ramadas

The Great Basin Indians spent much of their time outdoors. To protect themselves from the sun, they built a roofed shelter called a **ramada**. A ramada was simpler than a wickiup. It had a brush roof supported by four poles.

People sat under a ramada during the day. The ramada was often a place to rest and visit. It was also a place for children to play.

◄ A ramada was a simple shelter. It protected people from the sun.

Shelter for Travelers

The Great Basin Indians set up camps throughout the year. They did not view their wickiups as a home. Home was a group of valleys or a broad desert.

Wickiups were shelters used long ago. The Great Basin and Apache Indians no longer need these simple shelters. They do not move from place to place. Today, some people still build wickiups. They build wickiups to share the history of the Great Basin and Apache Indians.

◄ Wickiups were unlike other dwellings. People used them as shelters. They did not view them as a home.

Glossary

band (BAND)—a group of people smaller than a tribe

frame (FRAYME)—several wood poles that are tied together to make the base of a wickiup

Great Basin (GRAYT BAY-suhn)—a large desert region in the western United States; the basin covers land in Nevada and parts of Utah, California, Idaho, Wyoming, and Oregon.

ramada (ruh-MAH-duh)—a shelter built with four poles supporting a roof made of brush

temporary (TEM-puh-rer-ee)—lasting only for a short time

tribe (TRIBE)—a group of people who share the same ancestors, customs, and laws

twine (TWINE)—a strong rope made of two or more strands twisted together

Read More

Kalman, Bobbie. *Native Homes.* Native Nations of North America. St. Catharines, Ont.: Crabtree, 2001.

Mitchell, Kevin M. *Wickiup.* Native American Homes. Vero Beach, Fla.: Rourke, 2001.

Internet Sites

FactHound offers a safe, fun way to find Internet sites related to this book. All of the sites on FactHound have been researched by our staff.

Here's how:
1. Visit *www.facthound.com*
2. Type in this special code **0736837280** for age-appropriate sites. Or enter a search word related to this book for a more general search.
3. Click on the **Fetch It** button.

FactHound will fetch the best sites for you!

Index